The Emerald of Europe,
it sparkled and shone
In the ring of this world,
the most precious stone.

IN PRAISE OF IRELAND

IN PRAISE OF IRELAND

Summersdale Publishers Ltd
46 West Street
Chichester
West Sussex
PO19 1RP
UK

www.summersdale.com

Printed and bound in the Czech Republic

ISBN: 978-1-84953-561-8

Substantial discounts on bulk quantities of Summersdale books are available to corporations, professional associations and other organisations. For details contact Nicky Douglas by telephone: +44 (0) 1243 756902, fax: +44 (0) 1243 786300 or email: nicky@summersdale.com.

IN PRAISE OF IRELAND

Paul Harper

summersdale

When Erin first rose from
the dark-swelling flood,
God bless'd the green island,
He saw it was good:
The Emerald of Europe,
it sparkled, it shone,
In the ring of this world
the most precious stone!

WILLIAM DRENNAN, FROM 'ERIN'

Never before, we may confidently say, has a single people emerged from such varied vicissitudes, stronger at the end in genius, in spiritual and moral power... richer in vital force, clearer in understanding, in every way more mature and humane... We see in Ireland a land with a wonderful past, rich in tradition and varied lore; a land where the memorials of the ages, built in enduring stone, would in themselves enable us to trace the life and progress of human history.

CHARLES JOHNSTON,
IRELAND, HISTORIC AND PICTURESQUE

'Oh, where's the Isle we've seen in dreams,
Our destined home or grave?'
Thus sung they as, by the morning's beams,
They swept the Atlantic wave.
And, lo, where afar o'er ocean shines
A sparkle of radiant green,
As tho' in that deep lay emerald mines,
Whose light thro' the wave was seen.
'Tis Innisfail – 'tis Innisfail!'
Rings o'er the echoing sea;
While, bending to heaven, the warriors hail
That home of the brave and free.

THOMAS MOORE, FROM 'SONG OF INNISFAIL'

W e... are no petty people. We are one of the great stocks of Burke; we are the people of Swift, the people of Emmet, the people of Parnell. We have created most of the modern literature of this country. We have created the best of its political intelligence.

WILLIAM BUTLER YEATS

A great deal, however, had happened to Ireland before the bogs began to grow on it at all. It had... been twice at least united to England... and twice severed from it again. It had been exposed to a cold so intense as to bleach off all life from its surface, utterly depriving it of vegetation, and grinding the mountains down to that scraped bun-like outline which so many of them still retain; had covered the whole country, highlands and lowlands alike, with a dense overtoppling cap of snow, towering often thousands of feet above the present height of the mountains, from which 'central silence' the glaciers crept sleepily down the ravines and valleys, eating their way steadily seaward, and leaving behind them moraines to mark their passage, leaving also longitudinal scratches, cut, as a diamond cuts glass, upon the rocks.

EMILY LAWLESS, *THE STORY OF IRELAND*

If you think that you know all about Ireland, you are probably wrong. It is an undiscovered country.

FRANK MATHEW, *IRELAND*

'This is Ireland, Finley. It's rough. It's wild. And it is holy.'

JENNY B. JONES, *THERE YOU'LL FIND ME*

I sat down near a bridge at the end of the green, between a tinker who was mending a can and a herd who was minding some sheep that had not been sold. The herd spoke to me with some pride of his skill in dipping sheep to keep them from the fly, and other matters connected with his work. 'Let you not be talking,' said the tinker, when he paused for a moment. 'You've been after sheep since you were that height' (holding his hand a little over the ground), 'and yet you're nowhere in the world beside the herds that do be reared beyond on the mountains. Those men are a wonder, for I'm told they can tell a lamb from their own ewes before it is marked; and that when they have five hundred sheep on the hills – five hundred is a big number – they don't need to count them or reckon them at all, but they just walk here and there where they are, and if one is gone away they'll miss it from the rest.'

JOHN MILLINGTON SYNGE, *IN WICKLOW AND WEST KERRY*

Céad míle fáilte
(Kay-d meal-a fawl-tja)
A hundred thousand welcomes

Connemara is a country of shadows: on the bright days they drift on the waters, for the tarns and the inlets are all under hills, and they roam on the mountains when the weather is dark. To love it, you must first understand the pleasure of pain. And if you love it, you will think of it dark; you will not remember the brief sunshine but the days when the mountains seem to exult in defiance or to glory in suffering. All the wild country beyond the wild Shannon seems lulled in an unnatural sleep on days when the wind is still and the sun is out. When the storms rave in the mountains, the west is awake.

FRANK MATHEW, *IRELAND*

Still green are thy mountains
and bright is thy shore,
And the voice of thy fountains is
heard as of yore:
The sun o'er thy valleys, dear
Erin, shines on,
Though thy bard and thy lover
forever is gone.

Nor shall he, an exile, thy glad
scenes forget –
The friends fondly loved, ne'er
again to be met –
The glens where he mused on
the deeds of his nation,
And waked his young harp with
wild inspiration.

Still, still, though between us
may roll the broad ocean,
Will I cherish thy name with the
same deep devotion;
And though minstrels more
brilliant my place may supply,
None loves you more fondly,
more truly than I.

J. J. CALLANAN, 'STANZAS TO ERIN'

When I die Dublin will be written in my heart.

JAMES JOYCE

Our two nations, divided by distance, have been united by history... And no country contributed more to building my own than your sons and daughters.

JOHN F. KENNEDY, ADDRESS BEFORE THE IRISH PARLIAMENT

They are going, going, going from the
valleys and the hills,
They are leaving far behind them
heathery moor and mountain rills,
All the wealth of hawthorn hedges
where the brown thrush sways and trills.

They are going, shy-eyed colleens and
lads so straight and tall,
From the purple peaks of Kerry, from
the crags of wild Imaal,
From the greening plains of Mayo and
the glens of Donegal.

They are leaving pleasant places,
shores with snowy sands outspread;
Blue and lonely lakes a-stirring when
the wind stirs overhead;
Tender living hearts that love them,
and the graves of kindred dead.

They shall carry to the distant land a
tear-drop in the eye
And some shall go uncomforted – their
days an endless sigh
For Kathaleen ní Houlihan's sad face,
until they die.

**ETHNA CARBERY, FROM 'THE PASSING OF
THE GAEL'**

Níl aon tinteán mar do thinteán féin.
(Neel ayne tin-tawn mar du hin-tawn fayne.)
There is no fireside like your own fireside.

Ireland is where strange tales begin and happy endings are possible.

CHARLES HAUGHEY

A woman melodiously crying 'Dublin Bay herrings' passed just as we came up to the door, and as that fish is famous throughout Europe, I seized the earliest opportunity and ordered a broiled one for breakfast. It merits all its reputation; and in this respect I should think the Bay of Dublin is far superior to its rival of Naples. Are there any herrings in Naples Bay? Dolphins there may be; and Mount Vesuvius, to be sure, is bigger than even the Hill of Howth; but a dolphin is better in a sonnet than at a breakfast, and what poet is there that, at certain periods of the day, would hesitate in his choice between the two?

WILLIAM MAKEPEACE THACKERAY, *THE IRISH SKETCH BOOK*

I'd wed you without herds,
without money or rich array,
And I'd wed you on a dewy morn
at day-dawn grey;
My bitter woe it is, love, that we
are not far away
In Cashel town, tho' the bare
deal board were our marriage
bed this day!

SAMUEL FERGUSON,
FROM 'CASHEL OF MUNSTER'

Wherever you go and
whatever you do,
May the luck of the Irish be
there with you.

IRISH BLESSING

Where glows the Irish hearth with peat
There lives a subtle spell –
The faint blue smoke, the gentle heat,
The moorland odours tell.

Of white roads winding by the edge
Of bare, untamèd land,
Where dry stone wall or ragged hedge
Runs wide on either hand.

To cottage lights that lure you in
From rainy Western skies;
And by the friendly glow within
Of simple talk, and wise,

And tales of magic, love or arms
From days when princes met
To listen to the lay that charms
The Connacht peasant yet,

There honour shines through
passions dire,
There beauty blends with mirth –
Wild hearts, ye never did aspire
Wholly for things of earth!

And still around the fires of peat
Live on the ancient days;
There still do living lips repeat
The old and deathless lays.

And when the wavering wreaths ascend
Blue in the evening air,
The soul of Ireland seems to bend
Above her children there.

T. W. ROLLESTON, 'COIS NA TEINEADH'
(BESIDE THE FIRE)

The Irish love telling stories, and we are suspicious of people who don't have long, complicated conversations.

MAEVE BINCHY

Whenever something negative happens, there is always somebody quick with a smart remark to relax the mood.

CECILIA AHERN ON IRISH HUMOUR

I have come out again on the mountain road the third day of the fog. At first it was misty only, and then a cloud crept up the water gullies from the valley of the Liffey, and in a moment I am cut off in a white silent cloud. The little turfy ridges on each side of the road have the look of glens to me, and every block of stone has the size of a house. The cobwebs on the furze are like a silvery net, and the silence is so great and queer, even weasels run squealing past me on the side of the road... An east wind is rising.

JOHN MILLINGTON SYNGE, *IN WICKLOW AND WEST KERRY*

I found in Innisfail the fair,
In Ireland, while in exile there,
Women of worth, both grave and gay men,
Many clerics and many laymen.

I travelled its fruitful provinces round,
And in every one of the five I found,
Alike in church and in palace hall,
Abundant apparel, and food for all.

Gold and silver I found, and money,
Plenty of wheat and plenty of honey;
I found God's people rich in pity,
Found many a feast and many a city.

I also found in Armagh, the splendid,
Meekness, wisdom, and
prudence blended,
Fasting, as Christ hath recommended,
And noble councillors untranscended.

**ALDFRID, SEVENTH-CENTURY KING OF THE
NORTHUMBRIAN SAXONS, FROM 'PRINCE
ALDFRID'S ITINERARY THROUGH IRELAND'**

Éirinn go brách
(Erin guh brawk)
Ireland forever

How did you welcome May Morning, and how do you purpose to celebrate the birth-day of summer? Have you danced to the elfin pipers that played under the thorns of the Phoenix last night? Did you leap through the bonfires that blazed upon Tallaght and Harold's-cross Green? Were you out yester-eve to welcome the 'Young May Moon'? or up before sunrise this morning to gather the maiden dew from the sparkling gossamer, to keep the freckles off your pretty faces?

WILLIAM WILDE, *IRELAND: HER WIT, PECULIARITIES AND POPULAR SUPERSTITIONS*

The road was very agreeable. It began
with the Phoenix Park, and followed
the course of the Liffey, the river
which flows through Dublin, where its
beautiful quays, stone and iron bridges,
add so much to the embellishment of
the town... I asked a beggar whom I met,
how far it was to W– park, and whether
the road continued equally beautiful
all the way. 'Long life to your honour!'
exclaimed he, with Irish patriotism,
'only keep right on, and you never saw
anything more beautiful in this world!'

HERMANN VON PÜCKLER-MUSKAU, *TOURING
ENGLAND, IRELAND AND FRANCE IN THE YEARS
1826, 1827, 1828 AND 1829*

The groves of Blarney they are so charming
All by the purling of sweet silent streams;
Being banked with posies that
    spontaneous grow there,
Planted in order by the sweet rock close.
'Tis there the daisy, and the
    sweet carnation,
The blooming pink, and the rose so fair;
The daffodowndilly, besides the lily, –
Flowers that scent the sweet fragrant air.

RICHARD ALFRED MILLIKEN,
FROM 'THE GROVES OF BLARNEY'

'I am of Ireland,
And the Holy Land of Ireland,
And time runs on,' cried she.
'Come out of charity,
Come dance with me in Ireland.'

One man, one man alone
In that outlandish gear,
One solitary man
Of all that rambled there
Had turned his stately head.
'That is a long way off,
And time runs on,' he said,
'And the night grows rough.'

'I am of Ireland,
And the Holy Land of Ireland,
And time runs on,' cried she.
'Come out of charity
And dance with me in Ireland.'

WILLIAM BUTLER YEATS,
FROM 'I AM OF IRELAND'

The tune was sad, as the best of Ireland was, melancholy and lovely as a lover's tears.

NORA ROBERTS, *BORN IN FIRE*

To those who have seen the Irish lakes, the word Killarney is 'a joy for ever'.

SAMUEL REYNOLDS HOLE, *A LITTLE TOUR IN IRELAND*

I am a wand'ring minstrel man,
And Love my only theme,
I've stray'd beside the pleasant Bann,
And eke the Shannon's stream;
I've pip'd and play'd to wife and maid
By Barrow, Suir, and Nore,
But never met a maiden yet
Like *Brighidín bán mo stóre.*

My girl hath ringlets rich and rare,
By Nature's fingers wove –
Loch-Carra's swan is not so fair
As is her breast of love;
And when she moves, in Sunday sheen,
Beyond our cottage door,
I'd scorn the high-born Saxon queen
For *Bríghidín bán mo stóre.*

EDWARD WALSH, FROM 'BRÍGHIDÍN BÁN MO
STÓRE' (BRIDGET, MY TREASURE)

The first thing to note is that in my son's veins flowed the blood of Irish rebels.

ERNESTO GUEVARA, ON HIS SON CHE GUEVARA

You cannot conquer Ireland. You cannot extinguish the Irish passion for freedom.

PÁDRAIG PEARSE, ON THE EASTER RISING

Erin! an exile bequeaths thee
his blessing!
Land of my forefathers, *Erin-go-bragh*!
Buried and cold when my heart stills
her motion,
Green be thy fields, sweetest isle of
the ocean!
And thy harp-striking bards sing aloud
with devotion,
*Erin, mavournin, Erin-go-bragh!**

THOMAS CAMPBELL, FROM 'THE EXILE OF ERIN'

*Ireland, my darling, Ireland for ever!

A view of singular magnificence here bursts upon you – a view that of its kind is probably unequalled in the British Isles. The lofty mountain of Slieve League gives on the land side no promise of the magnificence that it presents from the sea, being in fact, a mural precipice of one thousand nine hundred and seventy-two feet in height, descending to the water's edge in one superb escarpment. And not only in its height is it so sublime, but in the glorious colours which are grouped in masses on its face. Stains of metals green, amber, gold, yellow, white, red – and every variety of shade are observable, particularly when seen under a bright sun, contrasting in a wonderful manner with the dark-blue waters beneath. In cloudy or stormy weather this peculiarity is to a certain degree lost, though other effects take its place and render it even more magnificent.

SAMUEL G. BAYNE, *ON AN IRISH JAUNTING-CAR THROUGH DONEGAL AND CONNEMARA*

Prince Philip and I are delighted to be here and to experience at first-hand Ireland's world-famous hospitality.

ELIZABETH II, FROM A SPEECH MADE DURING AN
IRISH STATE DINNER

Now sweetly lies old Ireland
Emerald green beyond
the foam,
Awakening sweet memories,
Calling the heart back home.

IRISH BLESSING

We see in Ireland a land full of a singular fascination and beauty, where even the hills and rivers speak not of themselves but of the spirit which builds the worlds; a beauty, whether in brightness or gloom, finding its exact likeness in no other land; we see all this, but we see much more: not a memory of the past, but a promise of the future; no offering of earthly wealth, but rather a gift to the soul of man; not for Ireland only, but for all mankind.

CHARLES JOHNSTON, *IRELAND, HISTORIC AND PICTURESQUE*

Dear lovely bowers of innocence and ease,
Seats of my youth, where every sport
could please,
How often have I loitered o'er thy green,
Where humble happiness endeared
each scene;
How often have I paused on every charm,
The sheltered cot, the cultivated farm,
The never-failing brook, the busy mill,
The decent church that topped the
neighbouring hill,
The hawthorn bush, with seats beneath
the shade,
For talking age and whispering
lovers made.

OLIVER GOLDSMITH,
FROM 'THE DESERTED VILLAGE'

The great Gaels of Ireland
Are the men that God
made mad,
For all their wars are merry,
And all their songs are sad.

G. K. CHESTERTON, *THE BALLAD OF THE
WHITE HORSE*

The last time I traversed the valley it was moonlight, and I should have found my way with difficulty but for a young man who was returning from shooting; with true Irish kindness and courtesy he accompanied me at least three miles on foot, far beyond the most intricate parts. The night was extremely clear and mild, the sky as blue as by day, and the moon lustrous as a gem. Though I lost something in extent of view, I gained perhaps more by the magic light which was diffused through the atmosphere; by the darker and more fantastic contours of the rocks, the thought-pregnant stillness, and the sweetly-awful loneliness of night.

HERMANN VON PÜCKLER-MUSKAU, *TOURING ENGLAND, IRELAND AND FRANCE IN THE YEARS 1826, 1827, 1828 AND 1829*, ON AVONDALE, COUNTY WICKLOW

Oh, Danny boy, the pipes, the
pipes are calling
From glen to glen, and down the
mountain side
The summer's gone, and all the
roses are falling,
It's you, it's you must go and
I must bide.

But come ye back when summer's
in the meadow,
Or when the valley's hushed and
white with snow,
It's I'll be here in sunshine or in
shadow,
Oh, Danny boy, oh, Danny boy, I
love you so!

But when ye come, and all the
flowers are dying,
If I am dead, as dead I well may
be,
Ye'll come and find the place
where I am lying,
And kneel and say an 'Ave' there
for me.

And I shall hear, though soft you
tread above me,
And all my grave will warmer,
sweeter be,
For you will bend and tell me that
you love me,
And I shall sleep in peace until
you come to me!

FREDERIC EDWARD WEATHERLY, 'DANNY BOY'

Ireland is rich in literature that understands a soul's yearnings, and dancing that understands a happy heart.

MARGARET JACKSON

Maybe it's bred in the bone, but the sound of pipes is a little bit of heaven to some of us.

NANCY O'KEEFE

When you see the proudest of all, Dunluce Castle, looming out of the mist from its high separated rock, you might easily think it a part of the ruined sea wall beside it. You might imagine that only a Giant could have planted it there.

FRANK MATHEW, *IRELAND*

A plenteous place is Ireland for
hospitable cheer,
Uileacan dubh O!
Where the wholesome fruit is bursting
from the yellow barley ear;
Uileacan dubh O!
There is honey in the trees where her
misty vales expand,
And her forest paths, in summer, are
by falling waters fann'd,
There is dew at high noontide there,
and springs i' the yellow sand,
On the fair hills of holy Ireland.

[...]

Large and profitable are the stacks
upon the ground,
Uileacan dubh O!
The butter and the cream do
wondrously abound;
Uileacan dubh O!
The cresses on the water and the
sorrels are at hand,
And the cuckoo's calling daily his note
of mimic bland,
And the bold thrush sings so bravely
his song i' the forests grand,
On the fair hills of holy Ireland.

SAMUEL FERGUSON,
FROM 'THE FAIR HILLS OF IRELAND'

No land in the world can inspire such love in a common man.

FRANK DELANEY, *IRELAND*

Moderation, we find, is an extremely difficult thing to get in this country.

FLANN O'BRIEN, *THE BEST OF MYLES*

When anyone asks me about the Irish character, I say look at the trees. Maimed, stark and misshapen, but ferociously tenacious.

EDNA O'BRIEN

'It would be delightful Son of my God, to travel over the waves of the rising flood; over Loch Neach, over Loch Febhail, beyond Beinn Eigne, the place we used to hear fitting music from the swans... in the strange country where I have chanced... to listen at break of day to the lowing of the cattle in Rigrencha, to listen at the brink of summer to the cry of the cuckoo from the tree... I have loved Ireland of the waters, all that is in it.'

AUGUSTA, LADY GREGORY, *A BOOK OF SAINTS AND WONDERS PUT DOWN HERE*, QUOTING A HYMN BY ST COLUMCILLE OF IONA

Being Irish, he had an abiding sense of tragedy, which sustained him through temporary periods of joy.

WILLIAM BUTLER YEATS

I'm Irish and the Irish are very emotionally moved. My mother is Irish and she cries during beer commercials.

BARRY MCCAFFREY

I was elected by the women of Ireland, who instead of rocking the cradle, rocked the system.

MARY ROBINSON

We pleased ourselves with the spectacle of Dublin's commerce – the barges signalled from far away by their curls of woolly smoke, the brown fishing fleet beyond Ringsend, the big white sailing-vessel which was being discharged on the opposite quay. Mahony said it would be right skit to run away to sea on one of those big ships, and even I, looking at the high masts, saw, or imagined, the geography which had been scantily dosed to me at school gradually taking substance under my eyes.

JAMES JOYCE,
THE DUBLINERS, 'AN ENCOUNTER'

Ireland lies the last outpost of Europe against the vast flood of the Atlantic Ocean; unlike all other islands it is circled round with mountains, whose precipitous cliffs rising sheer above the water stand as bulwarks thrown up against the immeasurable sea.

ALICE STOPFORD GREEN, *IRISH NATIONALITY*

The music of ancient Ireland consisted wholly of short airs, each with two strains or parts – seldom more. But these, though simple in comparison with modern music, were constructed with such exquisite art that of a large proportion of them it may be truly said no modern composer can produce airs of a similar kind to equal them.

PATRICK WESTON JOYCE, *A SMALLER SOCIAL HISTORY OF ANCIENT IRELAND*

Dear Harp of my Country!
in darkness I found thee,
The cold chain of silence had
hung o'er thee long,
When proudly, my own Island Harp,
I unbound thee,
And gave all thy chords to light,
freedom, and song!
The warm lay of love and the light
note of gladness
Have waken'd thy fondest, thy
liveliest thrill;
But, so oft hast thou echoed the
deep sigh of sadness,
That e'en in thy mirth it will steal
from thee still.

Dear Harp of my Country!
farewell to thy numbers,
This sweet wreath of song is the
last we shall twine!
Go, sleep with the sunshine of
Fame on thy slumbers,
Till touched by some hand less
unworthy than mine.
If the pulse of the patriot, soldier,
or lover,
Have throbbed at our lay, 'tis thy
glory alone;
I was but as the wind, passing
heedlessly over,
And all the wild sweetness I
waked was thy own.

Thomas Moore, 'Dear Harp of my Country'

Ireland is like nowhere else. Ireland is magnificent, mischievous, moody and misunderstood.

CHRISTOPHER WINN, *I NEVER KNEW THAT ABOUT IRELAND*

Good puzzle would be cross Dublin without passing a pub.

JAMES JOYCE, *ULYSSES*

May the Irish hills
caress you.
May her lakes and rivers
bless you.
May the luck of the Irish
enfold you.
May the blessings of Saint
Patrick behold you.

IRISH BLESSING

I've been a wild rover for many's a year
And I've spent all my money
on whiskey and beer
And now I'm returnin' with
gold in great store
And I never will play the
wild rover no more.

And it's No! Nay! Never!
No nay never no more
And I'll play the wild rover
No never no more.

I went to an alehouse I used to frequent
And I told the landlady
my money was spent
I asked her for credit,
she answered me nay
Saying, 'Custom like yours
I can have any day!'

And it's No! Nay! Never!
No nay never no more
And I'll play the wild rover
No never no more.

I took from my pocket ten
    sovereigns bright
And the landlady's eyes opened
    wide with delight
She said, 'I have whiskeys and
    wines of the best
And the words that I told you
    were only in jest.'

And it's No! Nay! Never!
No nay never no more
And I'll play the wild rover
No never no more.

I'll go home to my parents,
confess what I've done
And I'll ask them to pardon
their prodigal son
And when they have kissed
me as oft-times before
I never will play the wild rover no more.

And it's No! Nay! Never!
No nay never no more
And I'll play the wild rover
No never no more.

'THE WILD ROVER', TRADITIONAL IRISH SONG

Go n'éirí an t-ádh leat
(Gu nigh ree on taw lath)
May luck rise with you

I have heard some capital music... that sort which is used, namely, to set young people dancing, which they have done merrily for some nights. In respect of drinking, among the gentry teetotalism does not, thank heaven I as yet appear to prevail; but although the claret has been invariably good, there has been no improper use of it. Let all English be recommended to be very careful of whiskey, which experience teaches to be a very deleterious drink. Natives say that it is wholesome, and may be sometimes seen to use it with impunity; but the whiskey-fever is naturally more fatal to strangers than inhabitants of the country; and whereas an Irishman will sometimes imbibe a half-dozen tumblers of the poison, two glasses will be often found to cause headaches, heartburns, and fevers to a person newly arrived in the country.

WILLIAM MAKEPEACE THACKERAY, *THE IRISH SKETCH BOOK*

Those who drink to forget, please pay in advance.

SIGN AT THE HIBERNIAN BAR, CORK CITY

I am a drinker with a writing problem.

BRENDAN BEHAN

It is what the poets of Ireland used to be saying, that every brave man, good at fighting, and every man that could do great deeds and not be making much talk about them, was of the Sons of the Gael; and that every skilled man that had music and that did enchantments secretly, was of the Tuatha de Danaan.

AUGUSTA, LADY GREGORY, *GODS AND FIGHTING MEN*

Blow softly down the valley,
O wind, and stir the fern
That waves its green fronds over
The King of Ireland's Cairn.

Here in his last wild foray
He fell, and here he lies –
His armour makes no rattle,
The clay is in his eyes.

His spear, that once was lightning
Hurled with unerring hand,
Rusts by his fleshless fingers
Beside his battle brand.

His shield that made a pillow
Beneath his noble head,
Hath mouldered, quite forgotten,
With the half-forgotten dead.

Say, doth his ghost remember
Old fights – old revellings,
When the victor-chant re-echoed
In Tara of the Kings?

Say; down those Halls of Quiet
Doth he cry upon his Queen?
Or doth he sleep contented
To dream of what has been?

Nay; nay, he still is kingly –
He wanders in a glen
Where Fionn goes by a-hunting
With misty Fenian men.

ETHNA CARBERY, FROM 'THE KING OF IRELAND'S CAIRN'

No nation is more poetical, or more richly endowed with fancy.

HERMANN VON PÜCKLER-MUSKAU, *TOURING ENGLAND, IRELAND AND FRANCE IN THE YEARS 1826, 1827, 1828 AND 1829*

It's not that the Irish are cynical. It's simply that they have a wonderful lack of respect for everything and everybody.

BRENDAN BEHAN

There is something uncanny about Ireland. Perhaps it is merely this impression of holiness, a thing rare enough now to seem uncanny; but be that as it may, one is apt to be conscious of some unnatural chill, as if the place was haunted... There is only one mournful Fairy, the Banshee, whose duty it is to give a warning of death by wailing in the night. Strictly speaking, she is not a Fairy but a supernatural being related to the usual ghost. She is described as a tall woman in white; but on this point the evidence is weak, for she is heard but not seen.

FRANK MATHEW, *IRELAND*

One morning early I went out
On the shore of Lough Leane
The leafy trees of summertime
And the warm rays of the sun
As I wandered through the townlands
And the luscious grassy plains
Who should I meet but a beautiful maid
At the dawning of the day.

No cap or cloak this maiden wore
Her neck and feet were bare
Down to the grass in ringlets fell
Her glossy golden hair
A milking pail was in her hand
She was lovely, young and gay
Her beauty excelled even Helen of Troy
At the dawning of the day.

On a mossy bank I sat me down
With the maiden by my side
With gentle words I courted her
And asked her to be my bride
She turned and said, 'Please go away'
Then went on down the way
And the morning light was shining bright
At the dawning of the day.

EDWARD WALSH, 'DAWNING OF THE DAY'
(FÁINNE GEAL AN LAE)

There's a dear little plant that
grows in our isle,
'Twas Saint Patrick himself sure that set it;
And the sun on his labour
with pleasure did smile,
And with dew from his eye often wet it.
It thrives through the bog, through the
brake, and the mireland;
And he called it the dear little
shamrock of Ireland –
The sweet little shamrock,
the dear little shamrock,
The sweet little, green little,
shamrock of Ireland!

That dear little plant still grows in our land,
Fresh and fair as the daughters of Erin
Whose smiles can bewitch,
whose eyes can command,
In each climate that they may appear in;
And shine through the bog, through
the brake, and the mireland;
Just like their own dear little
shamrock of Ireland.
The sweet little shamrock,
the dear little shamrock,
The sweet little, green little,
shamrock of Ireland!

That dear little plant that springs
from our soil,
When its three little leaves are extended,
Denotes from one stalk we
together should toil,
And ourselves by ourselves
be befriended;
And still through the bog, through the
brake, and the mireland,
From one root should branch, like the
shamrock of Ireland.
The sweet little shamrock,
the dear little shamrock,
The sweet little, green little,
shamrock of Ireland!

**ANDREW CHERRY, 'THE GREEN LITTLE
SHAMROCK OF IRELAND'**

Leprechauns, castles, good
luck and laughter,
Lullabies, dreams and
love ever after,
Poems and songs with
pipes and drums,
A thousand welcomes
when anyone comes,
That's the Irish for you!

IRISH BLESSING

Ireland is... our one doorway to the history of northern Europe through the long era of pagan times. That history was everywhere a fierce tale of tribal warfare. Its heroes are valiant fighters, keen leaders of forays, champion swordsmen and defenders of forts. The air throbs to the battle-drum, rings to the call of the war-trumpet.

CHARLES JOHNSTON, *IRELAND, HISTORIC AND PICTURESQUE*

This little country that inspires the biggest things – your best days are still ahead.

BARACK OBAMA, ON IRELAND

Long ago there dwelt in Ireland the race called by the name of De Danaan, or People of the Goddess Dana. They were a folk who delighted in beauty and gaiety, and in fighting and feasting, and loved to go gloriously apparelled, and to have their weapons and household vessels adorned with jewels and gold. They were also skilled in magic arts, and their harpers could make music so enchanting that a man who heard it would fight, or love, or sleep, or forget all earthly things, as they who touched the strings might will him to do.

T. W. ROLLESTON, *THE HIGH DEEDS OF FINN AND OTHER BARDIC ROMANCES OF ANCIENT IRELAND*

Good St Patrick travelled far, to teach
God's Holy Word,
And when he came to Erin's sod, a
wondrous thing occurred.
He plucked a shamrock from the earth
and held it in His hand,
To symbolise the Trinity that all
might understand.
The first leaf for the Father,
And the second for the Son,
The third leaf for the Holy Spirit,
All three of them in one.

'LEGEND OF SAINT PATRICK'

Wherever you go in Ireland you tread consecrated ground. Here among these mellow hills and serene valleys you find the restored domination of the primitive monks.

FRANK MATHEW, *IRELAND*, ON WICKLOW

There were many great saints among the Gael, but Patrick was the bush among them all... he went back to his own country, and his people asked him to stop there with them. But he would not; for always in his sleep he could see the island of the Gael, and he could hear the singing of the children.

AUGUSTA, LADY GREGORY, *A BOOK OF SAINTS AND WONDERS PUT DOWN HERE*

I gave myself to rummaging the scanty
knowledge I had of Ireland, to ascertain
whether I knew anything tolerable of its
true condition and character – and what
did I know?

I knew that between the parallels of
51 and 55 of north latitude there was a
little green spot in the ocean, defended
from its surging waves by bold defying
rocks; that over this spot are sprinkled
mountains, where sparkles the diamond
and where sleeps the precious stone;
glens, where the rich foliage and the
pleasant flower, and where the morning
song of the bird is blending with the

playful rill... I knew that proud castles and monasteries, palaces and towers, tell to the passer-by that here kings and chieftains struggled for dominion, and priests and prelates contended for religion; and that the towering steeple and the more lowly cross still say that the instinct of worship yet lives... I knew that no venomous serpent was lying in the path of the weary traveller, and that the purest breezes of heaven were wafted from mountain-top to lowly valley, giving health and vigour to the life-blood, and causing the 'inhabitants of the rock to sing'.

ASENATH NICHOLSON,
IRELAND'S WELCOME TO THE STRANGER

I live in Ireland every day in a drizzly dream of a Dublin walk.

JOHN GEDDES, *A FAMILIAR RAIN*

You know it's summer in Ireland when the rain gets warmer.

HAL ROACH

O Son of God, it would be sweet
a lovely journey
to cross the wave, the fount in flood
and visit Ireland.

The fields of Ireland I have loved
and that's no lie.
To stay with Comgall, to visit
Caindech
it would be sweet.

SAINT COLUMBA

Ireland, thou friend of my country in my country's most friendless days, much injured, much enduring land, accept this poor tribute from one who esteems thy worth, and mourns thy desolation.

GEORGE WASHINGTON, ON IRELAND'S SUPPORT FOR AMERICA DURING THE REVOLUTIONARY WAR

I see in Ireland a miraculous and divine history, a life and destiny invisible, lying hid within her visible life. Like that throbbing presence of the night which whispers along the hills, this diviner whisper, this more miraculous and occult power, lurks in our apparent life. From the very grey of her morning, the children of Ireland were preoccupied with the invisible world...

We shall first learn, and then teach, that not with wealth can the soul of man be satisfied; that our enduring interest is not here but there, in the unseen, the hidden, the immortal, for whose purposes exist all the visible beauties of the world. If this be our mission and our purpose, well may our fair mysterious land deserve her name: Inis Fail, the Isle of Destiny.

CHARLES JOHNSTON, *IRELAND, HISTORIC AND PICTURESQUE*

I will arise and go now, and go to Innisfree,
And a small cabin build there, of clay
and wattles made:
Nine bean-rows will I have there, a hive
for the honey-bee,
And live alone in the bee-loud glade.

And I shall have some peace there, for
peace comes dropping slow,
Dropping from the veils of the morning
to where the cricket sings;
There midnight's all a glimmer, and
noon a purple glow,
And evening full of the linnet's wings.

I will arise and go now, for always night and day
I hear lake water lapping with low sounds by the shore;
While I stand on the roadway, or on the pavements grey,
I hear it in the deep heart's core.

WILLIAM BUTLER YEATS, 'THE LAKE ISLE OF INNISFREE'

Rich and rare were the gems she wore,
And a bright gold ring on her
wand she bore;
But oh! her beauty was far beyond
Her sparkling gems, or snow-white wand.

'Lady, dost thou not fear to stray,
So lone and lovely through this bleak way?
Are Erin's sons so good or so cold,
As not to be tempted by woman or gold?'

'Sir Knight! I feel not the least alarm,
No son of Erin will offer me harm:
    For, though they love woman
        and golden store,
    Sir Knight! they love honour
        and virtue more!'

On she went, and her maiden smile
In safety lighted her round the green isle;
And blest for ever is she who relied
Upon Erin's honour and Erin's pride.

**THOMAS MOORE, 'RICH AND RARE WERE THE
GEMS SHE WORE'**

I n Ireland the inevitable
never happens and the
unexpected   constantly
occurs.

JOHN PENTLAND MAHAFFY

In Dublin's fair city,
Where the girls are so pretty,
I once met a girl called sweet Molly Malone,
As she wheeled her wheelbarrow,
Through the streets broad and narrow,
Crying, 'Cockles and mussels,
Alive, alive, oh!'

'Alive, alive, oh,
Alive, alive, oh,'
Crying, 'Cockles and mussels,
Alive, alive, oh!'

FROM 'COCKLES AND MUSSELS'

As we were approaching Glengesh, we met a young Donegal girl on the road. She was dressed in black serge, and, although her feet were bare, her figure was erect and her carriage very graceful. She swung along the road with charming abandon, and might have shone at a 'drawing room' in Dublin Castle, the embodiment, the quintessence of unconscious grace.

SAMUEL G. BAYNE, *ON AN IRISH JAUNTING-CAR THROUGH DONEGAL AND CONNEMARA*

The wild geese are ranging,
Head to the storm as they faced it before!
For where there are Irish their hearts
are unchanging,
And when they are changed, it is
Ireland no more!
Ireland no more!

RUDYARD KIPLING, FROM 'THE IRISH GUARDS'

Oh Ireland my first and only love
Where Christ and Caesar are hand
in glove!

JAMES JOYCE

The pale hills of Ireland have the beauty
of holiness. There is in it the peace of a
cloister; it is as quiet as a nun.

FRANK MATHEW, *IRELAND*

Irishmen! Irishmen! think what is Liberty,
Fountain of all that is valued and dear,
Peace and security, knowledge and purity,
Hope for hereafter and happiness here.

Nourish it, treasure it deep in your
inner heart,
Think of it ever by night and by day;
Pray for it! – sigh for it! – work for it! –
die for it!
What is this life and dear freedom away?

**DENIS FLORENCE MACCARTHY,
FROM 'IRELAND'S VOW'**

The pale moon was rising above
the green mountains,
The sun was declining beneath the
blue sea;
When I strayed with my love by
the pure crystal fountain,
That stands in the beautiful Vale
of Tralee.

**WILLIAM PEMBROKE MULCHINOCK, FROM 'THE
ROSE OF TRALEE'**

There is a beautiful phrase in one of the ancient manuscripts descriptive of the wonderful power of Irish music over the sensitive human organisation: 'Wounded men were soothed when they heard it, and slept; and women in travail forgot their pains.'

LADY SPERANZA WILDE, *ANCIENT LEGENDS, MYSTIC CHARMS, AND SUPERSTITIONS OF IRELAND*

Oh! did you ne'er hear of 'the Blarney',
That's found near the banks of Killarney?
    Believe it from me,
    No girl's heart is free,
Once she hears the sweet sound of
        the Blarney.
For the Blarney's so great a deceiver,
    That a girl thinks you're there,
        though you leave her;
    And never finds out,
    All the tricks you're about,
Till she's quite gone herself, – with
        your Blarney.

Oh! say, would you find this
same 'Blarney'?
There's a castle, not far from Killarney,
On the top of its wall –
(But take care you don't fall,)
There's a stone that contains all
this Blarney.
Like a magnet, its influence such is,
That attraction it gives all it touches;
If you kiss it, they say,
From that blessed day
You may kiss whom you please with
your Blarney.

SAMUEL LOVER, 'THE BLARNEY'

May your heart be warm and happy
With the lilt of Irish laughter
Every day in every way
And forever and ever after.

IRISH BLESSING

Cork blarney does not mean very much, beyond a pleasant desire to please: it is best explained by other words popular here, such as wheedling, deludthering, soothering. None of these denote any culpable guile.

FRANK MATHEW, *IRELAND*

The Irish gave the bagpipes to the Scots as a joke, but the Scots haven't seen the joke yet.

OLIVER HERFORD

All the islands, whether north or south, will have gently rounded backs, clothed in pastures nearly to the crest, with garments of purple heather lying under the sky upon their ridges. Yet for all this roundness of outline there will be, towards the Atlantic end of either army, a growing sternness of aspect, a more sombre ruggedness in the outline of the hills, with cliffs and steep ravines setting their brows frowning against the deep... Such is this land of Éire, very old, yet full of perpetual youth; a thousand times darkened by sorrow, yet with a heart of living gladness; too often visited by evil and pale death, yet welling ever up in unconquerable life.

CHARLES JOHNSTON, *IRELAND, HISTORIC AND PICTURESQUE*

In the long run, love always brings victory, love is never defeated. And, I could add, the history of Ireland proves that.

POPE JOHN PAUL II

I reland is a land of poets and legends, of dreamers and rebels.

NORA ROBERTS, *TEARS OF THE MOON*

Then the sun rose, and I could see lines of smoke beginning to go up from farmhouses under the hills, and sometimes a sleepy, half-dressed girl looked out of the door of a cottage when my feet echoed on the road. About six miles from Aughrim I began to fall in with droves of bullocks and sheep, in charge of two or three dogs and a herd, or with whole families of mountain people, driving nothing but a single donkey or kid. These people seemed to feel already the animation of the fair, and were talking eagerly and gaily among themselves. I did not hurry, and it was about nine o'clock when I made my way into the village, which was now thronged with cattle and sheep...

[The men] began looking at the lambs again, talking of the cleanness of their skin and the quality of the wool, and making many extravagant remarks in their praise or against them. As I turned away I heard the loud clap of one hand into another, which always marks the conclusion of a bargain.

JOHN MILLINGTON SYNGE, *IN WICKLOW AND WEST KERRY*

If you're lucky enough to be Irish, then you're lucky enough.

PROVERB

Of their quickness as to the humour there can be no doubt.

CHARLES DICKENS, ON HIS DUBLIN AUDIENCE

Farewell, then, O wild Donegal! and ye stern passes through which the astonished traveller windeth! Farewell, Ballyshannon, and thy salmon-leap, and thy bar of sand, over which the white head of the troubled Atlantic was peeping! Likewise, adieu to Lough Erne, and its numberless green islands, and winding river-lake, and wavy fir-clad hills! Goodbye, moreover, neat Enniskillen, over the bridge and churches whereof the sun peepeth as the coach starteth from the inn.

WILLIAM MAKEPEACE THACKERAY, *THE IRISH SKETCH BOOK*

A fair girl was sitting in the
greenwood shade,
List'ning to the music the spring
birds made,
When, sweeter by far than the birds
on the tree,
A voice murmur'd near her, 'Oh come,
love, with me,
In earth or air,
A thing so fair
I have not seen as thee!
Then come, love, with me.'

'With a star for thy home, in a
palace of light,
Thou wilt add a fresh grace to the
beauty of night;
Or, if wealth be thy wish, thine are
treasures untold,
I will show thee the birthplace of jewels
and gold.
And pearly caves,
Beneath the waves,
All these, all these are thine,
If thou wilt be mine.'

Thus whisper'd a Fairy to tempt the
fair girl,
But vain was his promise of gold and
of pearl;
For she said, 'Tho' thy gifts to a poor
girl were dear,
My father, my mother, my sisters
are here.
Oh! what would be
Thy gifts to me
Of earth, and sea, and air,
If my heart were not there?'

SAMUEL LOVER, 'THE FAIRY TEMPTER'

The fishermen of Connemara believe that an island not to be found by any voyage exists near their shore, and they call it the Other Country. That near and remote place is a symbol of Ireland. Giraldus Cambrensis wrote that Ireland 'was separated from the rest of the known world, and in some sort to be distinguished as another world'; and among its early names there were two that support that opinion, the Oldest Place and the Country at the End of the Earth.

FRANK MATHEW, *IRELAND*

The marketplace is all astir,
The sombre streets are gay,
And lo! a stately galleon
Lies anchored in the Bay –
The colleens shy, and sturdy lads,
Are swiftly trooping down,
To greet the Spanish sailors
On the quay of Galway Town.

ETHNA CARBERY, FROM 'A BALLAD OF GALWAY'

The sky, washed by the rain of last night, is pale greenish-blue, and joyful with the song of skylarks.

HILARY BRADT, *CONNEMARA MOLLIE: AN IRISH JOURNEY ON HORSEBACK*

The Celt, and his cromlechs, and his pillar-stones, these will not change much – indeed, it is doubtful if anybody at all changes at any time. In spite of hosts of deniers, and asserters, and wise men, and professors, the majority still are averse to sitting down to dine thirteen at table, or being helped to salt, or walking under a ladder, or seeing a single magpie flirting his chequered tail. There are, of course, children of light who have set their faces against all this, though even a newspaper man, if you entice him into a cemetery at midnight, will believe in phantoms, for everyone is a visionary, if you scratch him deep enough. But the Celt is a visionary without scratching.

WILLIAM BUTLER YEATS

The breeze was fresh, the morn was fair,
The stag had left his dewy lair,
To cheering horn and baying tongue
Killarney's echoes sweetly rung.

**SAMUEL LOVER, FROM 'MACCARTHY'S GRAVE:
A LEGEND OF KILLARNEY'**

The ground whereon we stand is sacred – consecrated by the footprints of our patron saint, hallowed by the dust of kings. Look abroad over the wide, undulating plains of Meath, or to the green hills of Louth: where, in the broad landscapes of Britain, find we a scene more fruitful and varied, or one more full of interesting heart-stirring associations? Climb this tower and cast your eye along the river. Look from the tall, pillar-like form of the Yellow Steeple at Trim, which rises in the distance, to where yon bright line marks the meeting of the sea and sky below the Maiden Tower at Drogheda, and trace the clear blue waters of the Boyne winding through this lovely, highly cultivated landscape, so rich in all that can charm the eye and awaken the imagination.

WILLIAM WILDE, *THE BEAUTIES OF THE BOYNE AND THE BLACKWATER*

We heard the thrushes by the shore
and sea,
And saw the golden stars' nativity,
Then round we went the lane
by Thomas Flynn,
Across the church where bones
lie out and in;
And there I asked beneath
a lonely cloud
Of strange delight, with one
bird singing loud,
What change you'd wrought in
graveyard, rock and sea,
This new wild paradise to
wake for me –
Yet knew no more than knew those
merry sins
Had built this stack of thigh bones,
jaws and shins.

JOHN MILLINGTON SYNGE, 'IN KERRY'

'Wild wit, invention ever new,' appear in high perfection amongst even the youngest inhabitants of an Irish cottage. The word wit... means not only quickness of repartee, but cleverness in action; it implies invention and address, with no slight mixture of cunning; all which is expressed in their dialect by the single word 'cuteness' (acuteness)... Mixed with keen satire, the Irish often show a sort of cool good sense and dry humour, which gives not only effect but value to their impromptus.

MARIA EDGEWORTH, *ESSAY ON IRISH BULLS*

Health and life to you;
The mate of your choice to you;
Land without rent to you,
And death in Eirinn.

IRISH BLESSING

A splendid place is London, with
golden store,
For them that have the heart and
hope and youth galore;
But mournful are its streets to
me, I tell you true,
For I'm longing sore for Ireland in
the foggy dew.

The sun he shines all day here, so
fierce and fine,
With never a wisp of mist at all to
dim his shine;
The sun he shines all day here
from skies of blue:
He hides his face in Ireland in the
foggy dew.

The maids go out to milking in
the pastures grey,
The sky is green and golden at
dawn of the day;
And in the deep-drenched
meadows the hay lies new,
And the corn is turning yellow in
the foggy dew.

Mavrone! if I might feel now the
dew on my face,
And the wind from the mountains
in that remembered place,
I'd give the wealth of London, if
mine it were to do,
And I'd travel home to Ireland and
the foggy dew.

KATHARINE TYNAN, 'THE FOGGY DEW'

There once was a demographic survey done to determine if money was connected to happiness and Ireland was the only place where this did not turn out to be true.

FIONA SHAW

The Irish love words and use as many of them in a sentence as possible.

ANNE McCAFFREY

Long live the Irish. Long live their cheer. Long live our friendship. Year after year.

IRISH BLESSING

After the spiritual powers, there is nothing in the world more unconquerable than the spirit of nationality... The spirit of nationality in Ireland will persist even though the mightiest of material powers be its neighbour.

GEORGE WILLIAM RUSSELL, *THE ECONOMICS OF IRELAND AND THE POLICY OF THE BRITISH GOVERNMENT*

Had I Limerick's gems and gold at will
to mete and measure,
Were Loughrea's abundance mine and
all Portumna's treasure,
These might lure me, might insure me
many and many a new love,
But O! no bribe could pay your tribe for
one like you, my true love!

JAMES CLARENCE MANGAN, FROM 'ELLEN BAWN'

I'll seek a four-leaved shamrock in all
the fairy dells,
And if I find the charmed leaves, oh,
how I'll weave my spells!
I would not waste my magic might on
diamond, pearl, or gold,
For treasure tires the weary sense, –
such triumph is but cold;
But I would play th' enchanter's part,
in casting bliss around, –
Oh! not a tear, nor aching heart, should
in the world be found.

**SAMUEL LOVER, FROM 'THE FOUR-LEAVED
SHAMROCK'**

The savage loves his native shore,
Though rude the soil and chill the air;
Well then may Erin's sons adore
Their isle, which Nature formed so fair!
What flood reflects a shore so sweet,
As Shannon great, or past'ral Bann?
Or who a friend or foe can meet,
So gen'rous as an Irishman?

JAMES ORR, FROM 'THE IRISHMAN'

May the blessing of light
Be on you, light without and
light within.

May the blessed sunlight
Shine on you and warm your
heart till it glows
Like a great peat fire, so that the
stranger may
Come and warm himself at it,
and also a friend.

And may the light shine out of
the eyes of you
Like a candle set in the windows
of a house
Bidding the wanderer to come in
out of the storm.

And may the blessing of the rain
Be on you – the soft sweet rain.
May it fall upon
Your spirit so that all the little
flowers may spring up
And shed their sweetness
on the air.

And may the blessing of
the great rains
Be on you, may they beat
upon your spirit
And wash it fair and clean
And leave there many a shining
pool where the blue
Of heaven shines, and
sometimes a star.

And may the blessing of the earth
Be on you – the great round earth.

May you ever have a friendly greeting
For them you pass as you're going
along the roads.

May the earth be soft
under you when
You rest upon it, tired at
the end of the day
And may it rest easy over you when
At the last you lie out under it;
May it rest so lightly over you that
Your soul may be out from
under it quickly
And up and off, and on
its way to God.

IRISH BLESSING

Dear Erin, how sweetly thy green
bosom rises,
An emerald set in the ring of the sea,
Each blade of thy meadows my faithful
heart prizes,
Thou queen of the west, the world's
cushla ma chree.*

JOHN PHILPOT CURRAN,
FROM 'CUSHLA MA CHREE'

*Pulse of my heart.

Through all the towns of Innisfail
I've wander'd far and wide;
But from Downpatrick to Kinsale,
From Carlow to Kilbride,
'Mong lords and dames of high degree,
Where'er my feet have gone,
My Mary, one to equal thee
I've never look'd upon;
I live in darkness and in doubt
Whene'er my love's away,
But, were the blessed sun put out,
Her shadow would make day!

'Tis she indeed, young bud of bliss,
　　And gentle as she's fair,
Though lily-white her bosom is,
　　And sunny-bright her hair,
And dewy-azure her blue eye,
　　And rosy-red her cheek, –
Yet brighter she in modesty,
　　More beautifully meek!
The world's wise men from north to south
　　Can never cure my pain;
But one kiss from her honey mouth
　　Would make me whole again!

SAMUEL FERGUSON, FROM 'MOLLY ASTORE'

Ireland, it's the one place
on earth
That heaven has kissed
With melody, mirth,
And meadow and mist.

IRISH BLESSING

If ever I'm a money'd man, I mean,
please God, to cast
My golden anchor in the place where
youthful years were pass'd;
Though heads that bow are black and
brown must meanwhile gather grey,
New faces rise by every hearth, and old
ones drop away
Yet dearer still that Irish hill than all
the world beside;
It's home, sweet home, where'er I roam,
through lands and waters wide.
And if the Lord allows me, I surely
will return
To my native Belashanny*, and the
winding banks of Erne.

**WILLIAM ALLINGHAM, 'THE WINDING BANKS
OF ERNE'**

*Ballyshannon

It's easy to love humanity when you're this far away from it.

DANIEL DAY LEWIS, WHILE LOOKING DOWN FROM THE MOUNTAINS OF COUNTY WICKLOW

Wine comes in at the mouth
And love comes in at the eye;
That's all we shall know for truth
Before we grow old and die.
I lift the glass to my mouth,
I look at you, and I sigh.

WILLIAM BUTLER YEATS, 'A DRINKING SONG'

I stretch my sight over the salt waters from the strong oaken planks; there is a big tear in my eye when I look back on Ireland; my mind is set upon Ireland, on Loch Lene of Magh Line; on the country of the men of Ulster; on smooth Munster and on Meath.

AUGUSTA, LADY GREGORY, *A BOOK OF SAINTS AND WONDERS PUT DOWN HERE*

Thence we came to 'Cushcam', at which village be it known that the turnpike-man kept the drag a very long time waiting. 'I think the fellow must be writing a book,' said the coachman... I wish I could relate or remember half the mad jokes that flew about among the jolly Irish crew on the top of the coach, and which would have made a journey through the Desert jovial. When the pike-man had finished his composition (that of a turnpike-ticket, which he had to fill), we drove on to Dungarvan.

WILLIAM MAKEPEACE THACKERAY, *THE IRISH SKETCH BOOK*

The pillar towers of Ireland, how
wondrously they stand
By the lakes and rushing rivers
through the valleys of our land;
In mystic file, through the isle, they lift
their heads sublime,
These grey old pillar temples, these
conquerors of time!

DENIS FLORENCE MACCARTHY, FROM 'THE
PILLAR TOWERS OF IRELAND'

There is no language like the Irish for soothing and quieting.

JOHN MILLINGTON SYNGE

The railway ride from Dublin [is] quite amazing; every cottage looks as if it had been white-washed the day before; and many with charming gardens.

CHARLES DICKENS

May you always walk in sunshine
May you never want for more
May Irish angels rest their wings
Right beside your door.

IRISH BLESSING

If you're interested in finding out more about our books, find us on Facebook at **Summersdale Publishers** and follow us on Twitter at **@Summersdale**.

www.summersdale.com